What's Wrong with Eating Meat?

by Barbara Parham

Illustrated by Andrea Carmen, and as signed.

DISCARD

Published by Ananda Marga Publications
854 Pearl Street
Denver, Colorado, 80203

3/97

Printed in the United States of America.
ISBN number: 0-884-79-009-X
Library of Congress Catalog Number: 79-52319

Second edition 1981

Those interested in learning more about Ananda
Marga, its service work, or meditation teachings,
may contact Ananda Marga, 854 Pearl Street,
Denver CO 80203, U.S.A.

Table of Contents

The first thing many people ask when they hear about the vegetarian diet is, "What's wrong with eating meat? Millions of people do it; why should I stop?"

There are very important reasons why it is preferable not to eat meat—not emotional or sentimental, but very convincing and scientific reasons. If you consider these points carefully, you will probably want to try a vegetarian diet from now on.

But our ancestors have always eaten meat, haven't they?

No! After much recent study and research, scientists have concluded that our early ancestors were vegetarians who ate no meat except during periods of extreme crisis. It was only during the last Ice Age, when their normal diet of fruits, nuts, and vegetables was unavailable, that the early humans had to start eating animal flesh in order to survive. Unfortunately the custom of eating meat continued after the Ice Age, either by necessity (like the Eskimos and tribes who live in the far north), through habit, through conditioning, or through lack of proper knowledge. However, throughout history there have been many individuals and groups of people who have realized the importance of a pure diet for health, mental clarity, or spiritual reasons and who have thereby remained vegetarians.

But isnt it natural for human beings to eat meat?

No! Scientists know that the diet of any animal corresponds to its physiological structure. Human physiology, bodily functions, and digestive system are completely different from those of carnivorous animals. According to diet we can divide vertebrate animals into three groups: meat eaters, grass-and-leaf eaters, and fruit eaters. Let us look closely at each and see where humanity fits in.

● MEAT EATERS

Carnivorous animals, including the lion, dog, wolf, cat, etc., have many unique characteristics which set them apart from all other members of the animal kingdom. They all possess a very simple and short digestive system — only three times the length of their bodies. This is because flesh decays very rapidly, and the products of this decay quickly poison the bloodstream if they remain too long in the body. So a short digestive tract was evolved for rapid expulsion of putrefactive bacteria from decomposing flesh, as well as stomachs with ten times as much hydrochloric acid as non-carnivorous animals (to digest fribrous

3

tissue and bones). Meat eating animals that hunt in the cool of the night and sleep during the day when it is hot do not need sweat glands to cool their bodies, they therefore do not perspire through their skin, but rather, they sweat through their tongues. On the other hand, vegetarian animals, such as the cow, horse, zebra, deer, etc., spend much of their time in the sun gathering their food, and they freely perspire through their skin to cool their bodies. But the most significant difference between the natural meat eaters and other animals is their teeth. Along with sharp claws, all meat eaters, since they have to kill mainly with their teeth, possess powerful jaws and pointed, elongated, "canine" teeth to pierce tough hide and to spear and tear flesh. They do NOT have molars (flat, back teeth) which vegetarian animals need for grinding their food. Unlike grains, flesh does not need to be chewed in the mouth to predigest it; it is digested mostly in the stomach and the intestines. A cat, for example, can hardly chew at all.

● GRASS-AND-LEAF EATERS

Grass-and-leaf-eating animals (elephant, cow, sheep, llama, etc.) live on grass, herbs, and other plants, much of which is coarse and bulky. The digestion of this type of food starts in the mouth with the enzyme ptyalin in the saliva. These foods must be chewed well and thoroughly mixed with ptyalin in order to be broken down. For this reason, grass-and-leaf eaters have 24 special "molar" teeth and a slight side-to-side motion to grind their food, as opposed to the exclusively up and down motion of carnivores. They have no claws or sharp teeth; they drink by sucking water up into their mouths as opposed to lapping it up with their tongue which all meat eaters do. Since they do not eat rapidly decaying foods like the meat eaters, and since their food can take a longer time to pass through, they have much longer digestive systems — intestines which are *ten times* the length of the body. Interestingly, recent studies have shown that a meat diet has an extremely harmful effect on these grass-and-leaf eaters. Dr. William Collins, a scientist in the New York Maimonedes Medical Center, found that the meat-eating animals have an "almost unlimited capacity to handle saturated fats and cholesterol". If a half pound of animal fat is added daily over a long period of time to a rabbit's diet, after two months his blood vessels become caked with fat and the serious disease called atheriosclerosis develops. Human digestive systems, like the rabbit's, are also not designed to digest meat, and they become diseased the more they eat it, as we will later see.

● THE FRUIT EATERS

These animals include mainly the anthropoid apes, humanity's immediate animal ancestors. The diet of these apes consists mostly of fruit and nuts. Their skin has millions of pores for sweating, and they also have molars to grind and chew their food; their saliva is alkaline, and, like the grass and leaf eaters, it contains ptyalin for predigestion. Their intestines are extremely convoluted and are *twelve times* the length of their body, for the slow digestion of fruit and vegetables.

● HUMAN BEINGS

Human characteristics are in every way like the fruit eaters, very similar to the grass eaters, and very *unlike* the meat eaters, as is clearly shown in the table below. The human digestive system, tooth and jaw structure, and bodily functions are completely different from carnivorous animals. As in the case of the anthropoid ape, the human digestive system is *twelve times* the length of the body; our skin has millions of tiny pores to evaporate water and cool the body by sweating; we drink water by suction like all other vegetarian animals; our tooth and jaw structure is vegetarian; and our saliva is alkaline and contains ptyalin for predigestion of grains. Human beings clearly are not carnivores by physiology — our anatomy and digestive system show that we must have evolved for millions of years living on fruits, nuts, grains, and vegetables.

Furthermore, it is obvious that our natural instincts are non-carnivorous. Most people have other people kill their meat for them and would be sickened if they had to do the killing themselves. Instead of eating raw meat as all flesh-eating animals do, humans boil, bake, or fry it and disguise it with all kinds of sauces and spices so that it bears no resemblance to its raw state. One scientist explains it this way: "A cat will salivate with hungry desire at the smell of a piece of raw flesh but not at all at the smell of fruit. If man could delight in pouncing upon a bird, tear its still living limbs apart with his teeth, and suck the warm blood, one might conclude that nature provided him with meat-eating instinct. On the other hand, a bunch of luscious grapes makes his mouth water, and even in the absence of hunger he will eat fruit because it tastes so good."

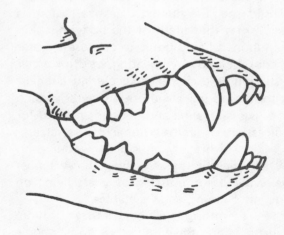

Scientists and naturalists, including the great Charles Darwin who gave the theory of evolution, agree that early humans were fruit and vegetable eaters and that throughout history our anatomy has not changed. The great Swedish scientist von Linne' states: "Man's structure, external and internal, compared with that of the other animals, shows that fruit and succulent vegetables constitute his natural food."

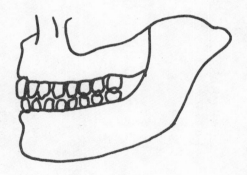

So it is clear from scientific studies that physiologically, anatomically, and instinctively, man is perfectly suited to a diet for fruit, vegetables, nuts, and grains. This is summarized in the following table.

	MEAT EATER	LEAF-GRASS EATER	FRUIT EATER	HUMAN BEINGS
1)	has claws	no claws	no claws	no claws
2)	no pores on skin; perspires through tongue to cool body	perspires through millions of pores on skin	perspires through millions of pores on skin	perspires through millions of pores on skin
3)	sharp, pointed front teeth to tear flesh	no sharp, pointed front teeth	no sharp, pointed front teeth	no sharp, pointed front teeth
4)	small salivary glands in the mouth (not needed to pre-digest grains and fruits)	well-developed salivary glands, needed to pre-digest grains and fruits	well-developed salivary glands, needed to pre-digest grains and fruits	well-developed salivary glands, needed to pre-digest grains and fruits

5)	acid saliva; no enzyme ptyalin to pre-digest grains	alkaline saliva; much ptyalin to pre-digest grains	alkaline saliva; much ptyalin to pre-digest grains	alkaline saliva; much ptyalin to pre-digest grains
6)	no flat back molar teeth to grind food	flat, back molar teeth to grind food	flat, back molar teeth to grind food	flat, back molar teeth to grind food
7)	much strong hydrochloric acid in stomach to digest tough animal muscle, bone, etc.	stomach acid 20 times less strong than meat-eaters	stomach acid 20 times less strong than meat-eaters	stomach acid 20 times less strong than meat-eaters
8)	intestinal tract only 3 times body length so rapidly decaying meat can pass out of body quickly	intestinal tract 10 times body length, leaf and grains do not decay as quickly so can pass more slowly through the body	intestinal tract 12 times body length; fruits do not decay as rapidly so can pass more slowly through the body	intestinal tract 12 times body length

History of Vegetarianism

From the beginnings of recorded history, we find that the vegetarian diet was regarded as the natural diet of humanity. The early Greeks, Egyptians, and Hebrews described man as a fruit eater. The wise priests of ancient Egypt never ate meat. Many great Greek wise men—including Plato, Socrates, and Pythagoras—were strong advocates of the vegetarian diet. The great civilization of the Inca Indians was based on vegetarian diet. In India the Buddha urged his disciples not to eat flesh. The Taoist saints and sages were vegetarians; the early Christians and Jews were also vegetarians. The Bible clearly states: "And God said, 'Behold, I have given you every herb-bearing seed, which is upon the face of the earth, and every tree, in which are fruits; for you it shall be as meat.' " (*Genesis* 1:29). St. Paul, one of the greatest disciples of Jesus, wrote in his letter to the Romans, "It is good not to eat flesh..." (*Romans* 14:21). Recently historians have discovered ancient texts similar to the *New Testament,* describing the life and speeches of Jesus. In one of these scriptures Jesus says: "And the flesh of slain beasts in a person's body will become his own tomb. For I tell you truly, he who kills, kills himself, and whosoever eats the flesh of slain beasts eats the body of death." (*The Essene Gospel of Peace*).

The ancient Hindus in India always forbade the eating of meat; the holy book of Islam, the Koran, prohibits the eating of "dead animals, blood, and flesh..." One of the first caliphs after Mohammed, his own nephew, advised the higher disciples, "Do not make your stomachs graves for animals."

So we see throughout history, many wise and knowledgeable people have adopted the vegetarian diet and have strongly urged others to do the same.

"Then said Daniel . . . 'Prove your servants, I beseech thee, ten days; and let them give us pulse to eat, and water to drink. Then let our countenances be looked upon before thee, and the countenance of the children that eat of the portion of the king's meat: and as thou seest, deal with thy servants.'

"So he consented to them in this manner, and proved them ten days. And at the end of ten days their countenances appeared fairer and fatter in flesh than all the children which did eat the portion of the king's meat." (*Daniel* 1:11-15)

What are the dangers of meat eating?

The Eskimos, living largely on meat and fat, age rapidly, with an average lifespan of 27½ years. The Kirgese, a nomadic Eastern Russian tribe that lived predominantly on meat, matured early and died equally early; they rarely passed the age of 40. In contrast, field investigations by anthropologists of non-meat cultures have documented the radiant health, stamina, and longevity enjoyed by people such as the Hunzas of Pakistan, the Otomi Tribe (Natives of Mexico), and Native peoples of the American Southwest. It is not uncommon for such tribes to have healthy and active individuals of 110 years *or more*. World health statistics consistently show that the nations which consume the most meat have the highest incidence of disease (heart, cancer), and groups of vegetarians in different countries have the lowest incidence of disease.

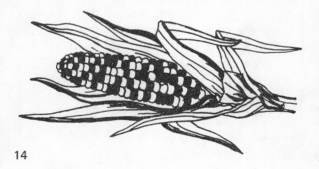

Why do meat eaters get more diseases and die sooner?

● **POISONING**

Just before and during the agony of being slaughtered, the biochemistry of the terrified animal undergoes profound changes. Toxic byproducts are forced throughout the body, thus pain-poisoning the entire carcass. According to the *Encylopedia Brittanica*, body poisons, including uric acid and other toxic wastes, are present in the blood and tissue:

"Protein obtained from nuts, pulses (lentils, peas, etc.), grains, and dairy products is said to be relatively pure as compared with beef with a 56% impure water content."

Just as our bodies become ill during times of intense rage or fear, animals, no less than humans, undergo profound biochemical changes in dangerous situations. The hormone level in the animals' blood — especially the hormone adrenalin — changes radically as they see other animals dying around them and they struggle futilely for life and freedom. These large amounts of hormones remain in the meat and later poison the human tissue. According to the Nutrition Institute of America, "The

15

flesh of an animal carcass is loaded with toxic blood and other waste byproducts."

● CANCER

A recent study conducted among 50,000 vegetarians (the Seventh Day Adventists) revealed results that shook the world of cancer research. The study clearly showed that this group has an astonishingly low rate of cancer. All types of cancer occurred at significantly lower rates as compared with a group matched on age and sex. The study showed that life expectancy of the Adventists is also significantly longer. A recent study of Mormons in California showed that cancer occurs in this group at a rate of 50% less than in the normal population. Mormons characteristically eat little meat.

Why do meat eaters get more cancer? One reason might be the fact that animal flesh which is several days old naturally turns a sickly grey-green color. The meat industry tries to mask this discoloration by adding nitrites, nitrates, and other preservatives. These substances make the meat appear red, but in recent years many of them have repeatedly been shown to be carcinogenic (cancer-inducing).

Said Dr. William Lijinsky, a cancer researcher at Oak Ridge National Laboratory in Tennessee, "I don't even feed nitrate-laden foods to my cat."

16

British and American scientists who have studied intestinal bacteria of meat eaters as compared to vegetarians have found significant differences. The bacteria in the meat eaters' intestines react with the digestive juices to produce chemicals which have been found to cause cancer. This may explain why cancer of the bowel is very prevalent in meat-eating areas like North America and Western Europe, while it is extremely rare in vegetarian countries such as India. In the United States, for example, bowel cancer is the second most common form of cancer (second only to lung cancer), and the people of Scotland, who eat 20% more beef than the English, have one of the world's highest rates of cancer of the bowel.

● CHEMICAL DIET

Eating meat has often been called "eating on top of the food chain." In nature there is a long chain of eaters: plants "eat" sunlight, air, and water; animals eat plants; larger animals or human beings eat smaller animals. Now, all over the world fields are being treated with poisonous chemicals (fertilizers and pesticides). These poisons are retained in the bodies of the animals that eat the plants and grasses. For instance, fields are sprayed with the insect-killing chemical DDT, a very powerful poison which scientists say can cause cancer, sterility, and serious liver disease. DDT and pesticides like it are retained in animal (and fish) fat and, once stored, are difficult to break down. Thus, as cows eat grass or feed, whatever pesticides they eat are mostly retained, so that when you eat meat, you are taking into your body all the concentrations of DDT and other chemicals that have accumulated during the animal's lifetime. Eating at the "top" (end) of the food chain, humans become the final consumer and thus the recipient of the highest concentration of poisonous pesticides. In fact, meat contains *13 times* as much DDT as vegetables, fruits, and grass. Iowa State University performed experiments which showed that most of the DDT in human bodies comes from meat.

But the poisoning of the meat does not stop here. Meat animals are treated with many more chemicals to increase their growth, fatten them quickly, improve their meat color, etc. In order to produce the most meat at the highest profit, animals are force-fed, injected with hormones to stimulate growth, given appetite-stimulants, antibiotics, sedatives, and chemical feed mixtures. The *New York Times* reported: "But of far greater potential danger to the consumer's health are the hidden contaminants — bacteria-like salmonella and residues from the use of pesticides, nitrates, nitrites, hormones, antibiotics, and other chemicals." (July 18, 1971). Many of these have been found to be cancer-causing chemicals, and, in fact, many animals die of these drugs even before they are led to slaughter.

As farms have evolved into animal factories, many animals never see the light of day — their lives are spent in cramped and cruel surroundings which culminate in a brutal death. A case in point is the high-rise chicken farms. According to an article in the *Chicago Tribune*, eggs are hatched on the top floor; the chicks are stimulated, drugged, and force-fed; they eat ravenously in their tiny cages — never getting exercise or fresh air. As they grow they are moved, one floor at a time, to lower levels. When they arrive at the bottom floor they are slaughtered. Such unnatural practices not only unbalance the body chemistry of the chickens and destroy their natural habits, but, unfortunately, the growth of malignant tumors and other malformations are quite common results.

● ANIMALS' DISEASES

Another danger facing meat eaters is that animals are frequently infected with diseases which are undetected or simply ignored by the meat producers or inspectors. Often, if an animal has cancer or a tumor in a certain part of its body, the cancerous part will be cut away and the rest of the body sold as meat. Or worse yet, the tumors themselves will be incorporated into mixed meats such as hot dogs, and euphemistically labeled "parts." In one area of America, where there is routine inspection of slaughtered animals, 25,000 cattle with eye cancers were sold as beef! Scientists have found experimentally that if the liver of a diseased animal is fed to fish, the fish will get cancer. A famous vegetarian doctor, Dr. J. H. Kellogg, once remarked when he sat down to a vegetarian dinner, "It's nice to eat a meal and not have to worry about what your food may have died of."

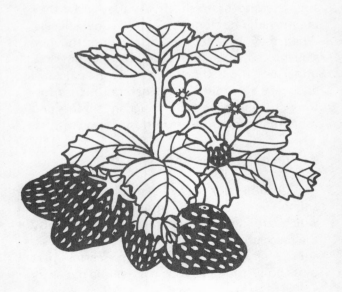

● HEART DISEASE

Perhaps the single most compelling argument for a non-meat diet, however, is the undeniable and well-documented correlation between meat eating and heart disease. In America (the highest meat consuming nation in the world) one person out of every two will die of heart or related blood vessel disease, whereas these diseases are practically unheard of in societies where meat consumption is low. The *Journal of the American Medical Association* reported in 1961 that "a vegetarian diet can prevent 90—97% of heart diseases (thromboembolic disease and coronary occlusions)."

What is it that makes meat so harmful to the circulatory system? The fats of animal flesh, such as cholesterol, do not break down well in the human body. These fats begin to line the walls of the meat eater's blood vessels. With the process of continual accumulation, the opening inside the vessels gets smaller and smaller as the years go by, allowing less and less blood to flow through. This dangerous condition is called atherosclerosis; it places a tremendous burden on the heart which has to pump harder and harder to send the blood through clogged and constricted vessels. As a result, high blood pressure, strokes, and heart attacks occur. Recently, scientists at Harvard found that the average blood pressure of vegetarians studied was significantly lower than that of a comparable group of non-vegetarians. During the Korean War, 200 bodies of young American soldiers, averaging about 22 years old, were examined after death. *Almost 80% had hardened arteries*, clogged with waste from eating meat. Korean soldiers of the same age group were examined and were found to be free of this damage to their blood vessels. The Koreans were basically vegetarians.

It is now recognized that the nation's number one killer, heart disease, has reached epidemic proportions. More and more physicians (and the American Heart Association) are sharply restricting the amount of meat that their heart patients can eat, or they are telling them to stop eating it entirely. Scientists now recognize that the roughage and fibre of vegetarian diets actually lower the level of cholesterol. Dr. U. D. Register, Chairman of the Department of Nutrition at Loma Linda University in California, describes experiments in which a diet rich in beans, peas, etc., actually reduced cholesterol, even while the subjects were eating large amounts of butter.

● PUTREFACTION

As soon as an animal is killed, proteins in its body coagulate, and self-destruct enzymes are released (unlike slow decaying plants which have a rigid cell wall and simple circulatory system). Soon, denatured substances, called ptomaines, are formed. Due to these ptomaines that are released immediately after death, animal flesh, fish, and eggs have a common property — extremely rapid decomposition and putrefaction. By the time the animal is slaughtered, placed in cold storage, "aged", transported to the butcher's shop, purchased, brought home, stored, prepared, and eaten, one can imagine what stage of decay one's dinner is in.

Meat passes very slowly through the human digestive system, which, as we have seen, is not designed to digest it. It takes meat about five days to pass out of the body (as opposed to vegetarian food, which takes only 1½ days), during this time the disease-causing products of decaying meat are in constant contact with the digestive organs. The habit of eating animal flesh in its characteristic state of decomposition creates a poisonous state in the

colon and wears out the intestinal tract prematurely.

Raw meat, being always in a state of decay, can contaminate cooks' hands and everything it comes into contact with. British public health officers, after an outbreak of food poisoning originating in slaughter houses, warned housewives to "handle raw meat as if it were hygienically equivalent to cow dung." Often poisonous bacteria are not destroyed even by cooking, especially if the meat is undercooked, barbecued, or roasted on a spit; these are notorious sources of infection.

● KIDNEY DISEASE, GOUT, ARTHRITIS

Among the most prominent wastes that a meat eater loads his body with are urea and uric acid (nitrogen compounds). Beefsteak, for example, contains about 14 grams of uric acid per pound. An American doctor analyzed the urine of meat eaters and vegetarians and found that the kidneys of meat-eaters have to do *three times* the amount of work to eliminate poisonous nitrogen compounds in meat than do the kidneys of vegetarians. When people are young, they are usually able to bear this extra burden so that no evidence of injury or disease appears; but, as the kidneys age and become worn out prematurely, they become unable to do their work efficiently, and kidney disease is the frequent result.

When kidneys can no longer handle the excessively heavy load of a meat-eating diet, the unexcreted uric acid is deposited throughout the body. There it is absorbed by the muscles like a sponge, soaking up water, and later it can harden and form crystals. When this happens in the joints, the painful conditions of gout, arthritis, and rheumatism result; when the uric acid collects in the nerves, neuritis and sciatica result. Now many doctors are advising patients suffering from these diseases to stop eating meat completely or to drastically reduce the amount they eat.

● POOR ELIMINATION

Since our digestive system was not designed for a meat diet, poor elimination is a natural consequence and distressingly common complaint of meat eaters. Meat, being extremely low in fiber, has this major disadvantage—it moves very sluggishly through the human digestive tract (four times slower than grain and vegetable foods) making chronic constipation a common ailment in our society.

Much recent research has shown conclusively that a healthy elimination pattern requires the bulk and fiber available only from a proper vegetarian diet. Vegetables, grains and fruits, in contrast to meat, retain moisture and bind bulk for easy passage. Vegetarians get generous portions of natural food fiber in their diet and benefit tremendously from the disease-preventative characteristics of this substance. According to present research, natural fiber may be a significant deterrent of appendicitis, diverticulitis, cancer of the colon, heart disease, and obesity.

Vegetarians are far healthier than meat eaters.

As we have seen, meat is not the natural or the most healthy diet for human beings. We can survive on it, of course, but it prematurely wears out the human body and creates many diseases. "A gasoline engine can operate on kerosene, but it will clog frequently, wear out sooner, and break down faster than if it were run on gasoline." And our bodies are not just machines, but intricate and beautiful creations which are to serve us our entire lifetime. It therefore stands to reason that they should be given the food which they were built to consume—a natural diet of fruit, grains, nuts, legumes, vegetables, and dairy products.

It is no wonder, then, that countless studies have proved that vegetarians all over the world are far healthier than those who eat meat.

● During the economic crisis of war, when people were forced to live on vegetarian diets, their health dramatically improved. In Denmark during World War I, there was a danger of an acute food shortage due to the British blockade. The Danish government appointed the director of the national vegetarian society to direct the rationing program. For the dura-

27

tion of the blockade the Danes were forced to subsist on grains, vegetables, fruits, and dairy products. In the first year of the rationing, the death rate fell 17%. When the people of Norway became vegetarians due to the food shortage of World War I, there was an immediate drop in the death rate from circulatory diseases. When the people of both Norway and Denmark returned to a meat diet after the war their death rate and heart disease rate promptly rose to pre-war levels.

● The Hunzas, a tribe in north India and Pakistan, have become internationally known for their freedom from disease and long life. Curious scientists from many lands have flocked to their villages to discover the secret of a culture where disease is almost unknown and natives often reach ages of 115 or more. Their diet consists mainly of whole grains, fresh fruits, vegetables, and goat's milk. Wrote Sir Rob McGarrison, a British general and doctor who worked with the Hunzas, "I never saw a case of appendicitis, colitis, or cancer."

● Recently, a group of Harvard doctors and research scientists went to a remote village of 400 people in the mountains of Ecuador. They were amazed to find that many of the native people lived to extraordinarily old ages. One man was 121 years old, and several were over 100. A thorough examination was given to those over the age of 75. Of these only *two* showed any evidence of heart disease! The villagers were pure vegetarians. The doctors called these findings "extraordinary" and said that "such examination of a similar population in the United States would show 95% with heart disease."

● Statistically, vegetarians in the United States are thinner and healthier. Over 50% of Americans are overweight, while on the average, vegetarians weigh about 20 pounds less than meat eaters. The American National Institute of Health, in a recent study of 50,000 vegetarians, found that the vegetarians live longer, have significantly lower incidence of heart disease, and have an impressively lower rate of cancer as compared to meat-eating Americans.

● In England vegetarians have to pay much less for life insurance than meat eaters because they are less likely to get heart disease and so are considered less of a risk by the insurance companies. And vegetarian restaurants pay less for their food poisoning insurance policies since their customers are much less likely to be poisoned by the food than restaurants which serve meat.

● At Harvard University a doctor has shown that a vegetarian diet reduces colds and allergies.

So it has been scientifically proven again and again that meat eating is positively harmful to the human body, while a well-selected vegetarian diet in harmony with the laws of nature will help us have a dynamically healthy body.

Vegetarians are more physically fit than meat eaters.

One of the greatest misconceptions about the vegetarian diet is that it will produce a weak, pale, sickly person. Nothing could be farther from the truth. Many studies, in fact, have shown vegetarians to be stronger, more agile, and to have more endurance than meat eaters.

● Dr. H. Schouteden at the University of Belgium conducted tests to compare endurance, strength, and quickness of recovery from fatigue in vegetarians and meat eaters. His findings indicated that vegetarians were substantially superior in all three characteristics.

● Dr. Irving Fisher of Yale University conducted endurance tests in 1906 and 1907. Yale athletes, instructors, doctors, and nurses participated in the study. His surprising evidence revealed that the vegetarians had nearly twice the stamina of meat eaters. Similar tests by J. H. Kellogg at Battle Creek Sanitarium in Michigan confirmed Fisher's findings.

● A study at Brussels University by Dr. J. Ioteyko and V. Kipani proved comparable to those of Dr. Fisher. In the endurance tests the vegetarians were able to perform two to three times longer than the meat eaters before complete exhaustion, and they took only one-fifth the time to recover from fatigue after each test than their meat-eating counterparts.

These striking results show that the vegetarian diet is superior for physical strength, endurance, and efficiency. Indeed, the world's most powerful and longest lived animals are all vegetarians. The horse, oxen, buffalo, and elephant all have the large, healthy bodies, the power of endurance, and the phenomenal strength that enables them to carry massive loads and do arduous work for man. None of the flesh-eating animals have the stamina or endurance to be beasts of burden.

It is also interesting to note how many great athletes who have set world records have been vegetarians.

● The Vegetarian Cycling Club in England has held over 40% of the national cycling records, and all over Europe the vegetarian cyclists have consistently made up a higher percentage of winners than the meat-eating cyclists.

● The great vegetarian swimmer, Murray Rose, was the youngest triple gold medal winner in the Olympic games. He has been hailed as one of the greatest swimmers of all time and has broken many records. A British vegetarian swam across the English channel faster than anyone in history — in 6 hours and 20 minutes.

● Many internationally famous athletes, past and present, changed to a vegetarian diet — for example, the Austrian weight lifter, A. Anderson, who won many world records, and Johnny Weismuller, who made 56 world swimming records. They report no decrease in strength; in fact, their ability seems to increase or stay the same.

● Bill Walton, the nationally acclaimed basketball star center, is famous for his aggressive, hard-driving performance. His personal experience has so convinced him of the benefits of a vegetarian diet that he has repeatedly advocated this regimen for others.

All over the world, vegetarians have set many records — in wrestling, boxing, walking, football, cross-country running, etc. Vegetarians actually have *more* endurance and energy because their bodies do not have to waste tremendous amounts of energy trying to counteract the poisons in meat.

Will I get enough nutrition without eating meat?

One of the worries people have when they think about adopting a vegetarian diet is, "Will I get enough nutrition if I don't eat meat? Will I get enough protein?" They have nothing to worry about, massive advertisement campaigns notwithstanding. A vegetarian diet can provide *all* necessary body nutrients. In fact, many studies have shown that a vegetarian diet provides much *more* nutritional energy than a meat diet.

We have been conditioned to believe that meat eating is necessary for health. In the 1950's scientists classified meat proteins as "first class" and vegetables as "second class." However, this idea has been completely disproved, because vegetable proteins have been found to be equally as effective and nutritious as meat proteins. The distinction is no longer made.

There is a tremendous range of protein content in vegetarian food, ranging from 8—12% in cereal grains to the incredibly protein rich soybean which has 40% protein, twice the amount found in meat. (Even the leanest cut of beefsteak has only 20% usable protein.) Many nuts, seeds, and beans are 30%.

35

The protein we need actually consists of 8 "essential" amino acids. Meat has often been purported to be superior because it has all 8 amino acids. What most meat eaters don't realize is that meat is not the only complete protein—soybeans and milk, for example, are also complete proteins. That is, they provide all the 8 amino acids we need, in the proper proportions.

Perhaps even more noteworthy is the fact that a complete protein is easily available simply by eating two of these (non-meat) foods together (such as rice and legumes), to make a high quality combination that far surpasses the protein value of either food alone. Poor people everywhere in the world seem to do this instinctively by mixing rice and tofu or beans (as in China and India), or corn and beans (as in Central and South America), etc.

In 1972 Dr. Frederick Stare of Harvard University conducted a comprehensive study of vegetarians (including adult men and women, pregnant women, and adolescent girls and boys). He found that all groups were consuming over twice their minimum daily protein requirement. In 1954 scientists conducted a detailed study at Harvard and found that when a variety of vegetable, grain, and dairy products were eaten in ANY combination there was always more than enough protein; they were unable to find a protein deficiency no matter what combinations were used. The scientists concluded that it is very difficult to eat a varied vegetarian diet which will *not exceed* protein requirements for the human body.

In newspapers we often read about the malnourished people in poor countries who are starving and dying from protein deficiency, and we often blame this on their vegetarian diet. But scientists have found that these people are undernourished not because they are not eating meat, but because they are not eating *enough* food. A diet of rice only (and very little of that) or sweet potatoes only, naturally leads to malnutrition and early death. By contrast, anywhere in this world that one can find people living on a vegetarian diet with an adequate caloric intake and an adequate variety of vegetables, grains, and legumes, there one will find strong, healthy, and thriving people.

We may do well to search for an explanation for the fact that we have been so thoroughly conditioned to believe we cannot possibly be healthy without eating large amounts of meat, when actually just the reverse is true. Who is perpetrating the "Great American Steak Religion," and why?

Is there any connection between our meat eating habits and world starvation?

Yes!

● If we conserved our grain supply and gave it to the poor and malnourished, instead of to cattle, we could easily feed nearly all of the chronically underfed people of the world.

● If we ate half as much meat, we could release enough food to feed the entire "developing world."

● A Harvard nutritionist, Jean Mayer, estimates that reducing meat production by just 10% would release enough grain to feed 60 million people.

● The shocking and tragic truth is that 80—90% of all grain grown in America is used to feed meat animals.

● Twenty years ago, the average American ate 50 pounds of meat annually; this year he will eat 129 pounds of *beef alone*. Because of America's "fixation on meat," most eat

38

twice the daily recommended protein allowance. Learning the real facts behind the "food shortage" is fundamental to an understanding of how we can properly utilize the world's resources.

More and more scientists and world economists are strongly advocating a vegetarian diet to solve the tremendous food problems of our planet, because, they say, eating meat is one of the main causes of these problems.

● BUT HOW DOES VEGETARIANISM RELATE TO FOOD SHORTAGE?

The answer is simple: meat is the most uneconomical and inefficient food we can eat; the cost of one pound of meat protein is *twenty times higher* than equally nutritional plant protein. Only 10% of the protein and calories we feed to our livestock is recovered in the meat we eat, that is, 90% goes "down the drain."

Vast acres of land are used to raise livestock for food. These acres of land could be utilized far more productively if planted with grains, beans, and other legumes for humans to eat directly. For example, one acre used to raise a steer will provide only about *one* pound of protein; but this same land planted with soybeans will produce *17* pounds of protein! In other words, to eat meat, we need to use

17 times as much land as the amount needed to plant soybeans. In addition, soybeans are more nutritious, contain less fat, and are free from the poisons of meat.

Raising animals for food is a tremendous waste of the world's resources not only of land, but also of water. It is estimated that raising food for a meat diet uses eight times as much water as growing vegetables and grains.

This means that while millions of people all over the world are starving, a few rich people are wasting vast amounts of land, water, and grain in order to eat meat, which is slowly

destroying their bodies. Americans consume over a ton of grain per person per year (through feed for meat-producing livestock), while the rest of the world averages about 400 pounds of grain.

United Nations Secretary General Kurt Waldheim has said that the food consumption of the rich countries is the key cause of the hunger around the world, and the United Nations has strongly recommended that these countries cut down on their meat consumption.

The primary solution to the global food crisis, many scientists are saying, is to gradually convert from a meat diet to a vegetarian diet. "If we were vegetarians, we could banish hunger from this earth. Children would be born and grow up well-nourished, and they would live happier, healthier lives. Animals would be free to live as wild, natural creatures, not forced to reproduce in great numbers as slaves to be fattened for the slaughter, with food that hungry people should be eating." (B. Pinkus, *Vegetable Based Proteins*).

"The earth has enough for everyone's need, but not enough for everyone's greed." (Mahatma Gandhi).

Because many scientists are saying that the bulk of future food needs will be met by plant proteins, several Western countries are currently financing much research to develop

41

delicious, vegetable-based proteins made from soy flour. But the Chinese people, among others, are way ahead of even this high level of research; they have been obtaining excellent protein by eating tofu and other soy products for thousands of years.

The vegetarian diet is the diet of the future—the diet which we human beings must adopt *once again* if we are to save our natural resources and, even more important, the precious lives of human beings all over the world. The vegetarian today is the human being of the future. Today's vegetarian points toward the direction that everyone will eventually follow, as people realize more and more the benefits of eating a vegetarian diet and the disastrous results of pursuing our present course.

Although meat production is surely a major contributor to the global food crisis, it is only a graphic representation of the underlying difficulty: an obscured yet pervasive pattern which permeates every aspect of the struggle to obtain basic needs of everyone on our planet.

The Politics of Hunger

According to a widely accepted myth about world hunger, the world does not have the capacity to feed its people. Everyone is doing the best they can, so the story goes. "There is simply not enough to go around. The hungry masses are rapidly multiplying, and if we are to avert disaster, a concerted effort to control population must be vigorously pursued."

However, a rapidly growing number of renowned scientists, economists, and agricultural experts are expressing their strong disagreement with this. "It is patently false — a myth," they say. "Actually there IS enough to go around, and then some. Any scarcities are due to wasteful utilization of resources and their irrational distribution."

According to Buckminster Fuller, there are enough resources at present to feed, clothe, house, and educate *every human being on the planet at American middle class standards*! Recent research by the Institute for Food and Development Policy has shown that there is no country in the world in which the people could not feed themselves from their own resources. There is no correlation between land density and hunger, they say. India is usually cited as the classic example of what happens when overpopulation occurs, and yet China has twice as many people per cultivated acre as India, and in China people are not hungry. Bangladesh has just one-half the people per cultivated acre that Taiwan has, yet Taiwan has no starvation while Bangladesh has one of the highest rates in the world. In fact, the most densely populated countries in the world today are NOT India and Bangladesh, but Holland and Japan. Clearly, population density is not the reason people starve. Of course the world *can* reach a limit of being able to support human population, but this limit is estimated to be about 40 billion (we are currently at 4 billion). Today more than half the world's people are *hungry all the time*; nearly half are starving. If there is enough to go around, where is it?

Let us take a look at who controls food and how it is controlled. The food industry is the largest in the world — to the tune of $150 billion a year (larger than auto, steel, or oil industries). A relatively few, giant multinational corporations dominate the industry; concentration of power is in their hands. It has become generally recognized and been well documented that giant corporations hold extensive political control; what this means is that a relatively few corporations are in a position to regulate and control the flow of food to billions of people. *How is this possible?*

● One of the ways giant corporations are able to control the market is gradually to take over every phase of the food system. For example, one giant corporation will produce farm machinery, feed, fertilizers, fuel, food contain-

Chris Scott
Courtesy of *Renaissance Universal Journal*

ers; it will buy chains of supermarkets, whole-sale businesses, and processing plants, and grow the food. A small farmer cannot compete with this because the corporation can artificially lower prices to undercut competition and drive the small farmer out of business, and it then more than recovers its losses by artificially raising the prices in areas where it has killed out the competition. Thus we see that since World War II the number of farms in the U. S. A. has dropped by half; more than 1,000 independent farmers are leaving their farms every week. And yet a U. S. Department of Agriculture study has recently shown that *small*, independent farms can produce food much more cheaply and efficiently than the giant agribusiness farms!

● Sheer economic strength: in the U. S., for example, less than one-tenth of one percent of all corporations own over 50% of all the corporate wealth. For instance, 90% of all grain marketing is controlled by only six companies.

● Power of decision: Agribusiness corporations decide what crops are to be produced, how much, what quality, and what price they are to be sold for. They have the power to hold back production or to store huge supplies of food, thereby creating artificial scarcities (which are notorious for raising prices).

● Governmental agencies that are supposed to regulate such matters are themselves dominated by agribusiness policy. Top governmental positions (Secretary of Agriculture, etc.) are regularly held by agribusiness' top corporation executives.

● Multinational giants have been extremely successful in achieving their goal of maximizing profits and amassing wealth. The rule of thumb is to increase prices as much as possible, while keeping production at the minimum necessary to sell the goods, so that in the short run prices fluctuate, but on a long range basis they only rise fairly rapidly.

● Multinationals are buying more and more land. A study of 83 countries revealed that just over 3% of land holders control about 80% of the farmland.

Although this pattern has meant great profits for a few, it has been a great detriment to many. There is no "land scarcity" or "food shortage" actually. If the goal were to utilize the resources of the world to meet humanity's needs, the goal could and would be easily met.

However, with a goal of maximum profits for a few, we have the tragic story of a planet with half its people hungry. Really speaking, the aspiration to become rich by exploiting others is a sort of mental malady — an ailment

47

that leads to all sorts of distortions on our earth:

● In Central America, where over 70% of the children are hungry, 50% of the land is used for "cash crops" (crops, such as lilies, which yield fast, big profits but are of little use for human survival). While multinational corporations use the best land to grow their cash crops (coffee, tea, tobacco, exotic foods), the domestic people are forced to use slopes and eroded land on which it is difficult to grow food.

● Development funds have irrigated the desert in Senegal so that multinational firms can grow eggplant and mangos for air-freighting to Europe's best tables.

● In Haiti the majority of (utterly impoverished) peasants struggle for survival by trying to grow food on mountain slopes of a 45° incline or more. They say they are exiles from their birthright — some of the world's richest agricultural land. These lands now belong to a handful of elite; cattle are flown in by U. S. firms for grazing and re-exported to franchised hamburger restaurants.

● In Mexico, land that was once used for growing corn for Mexicans is now used for the production of fancy vegetables for U. S. citizens; the profit is 20 times greater. Hundreds of thousands of former farmers have found themselves landless. Unable to compete with large landowners, they first lease their land to make at least *some* money from it; the next step is to work for the big firms; finally they find themselves migrant workers, roaming in search of work so their families can survive. Such conditions have led to repeated waves of rebellion.

● In 1975, Colombia's best soil was used to produce 18 million dollars of flowers. Carnations brought 80 times greater profit than did the former crop, wheat.

Not enough to go around? Hardly. The good land, the best resource, is being used to produce luxury crops for profit. Throughout much of the world we find a consistent, pervasive pattern. Agriculture, once the livelihood of millions of self-supporting farmers, is being turned into the production sites of high-profit non-essentials for the (well-fed) minority who can pay. Contrary to widespread myths, our food security is not being threatened by the prolific, hungry masses but by elites that profit by the concentration and internationalization of control of food resources.

Meat production is the epitome of this pervasive system. "The poor man's grain is being siphoned to feed the rich man's cow,"

49

says the director of the United Nations Protein Advisory group. As the demand for meat increases, rich nations are buying more and more grain to feed pigs and cattle. Grain supplies, once used to feed people, are sold to the highest bidder, and countless human beings are effectively condemned to starvation. "The wealthy can compete for the poor man's food; the poor cannot compete at all."

In a "Final Note to Consumers," John Powell of Food Education for Action writes: "The price of food will probably go up this summer, despite the fact that the price of grain has dropped 50% since 1973, which your food bill has not yet reflected. But, in looking for the reasons for this increase, don't just look at Arabs and the price of oil and booming population in the Third World. Look to the multinational corporations that control food industry with a little help from their friends in government. And remember, they are in the business

> "When the whole property of this universe has been inherited by all creatures, how then can there be any justification for a system in which someone receives a flow of huge excess, while others die for lack of a handful of grains."
>
> P. R. Sarkar

of making money, not feeding people. And while we are trying to explode myths, let's remember, we are not helpless."

Indeed we are not helpless. And even though the difficulties facing humanity may seem almost insurmountable, many people feel that we are at the threshhold of a new era, when human beings everywhere will recognize the simple truth that human society is One and indivisible; thus the suffering of one implies the suffering of all.

In discussing how a society based on universalism can be established, P. R. Sarkar explains: "A harmonious society can be achieved by *mobilizing the living spirit* of those who desire to establish one human society...those at the forefront of such a moral movement will be leaders of moral integrity, leaders whose goal is not fame or wealth or power but the interests of the whole human society."

"Just as the advent of the crimson dawn is inevitable at the end of the cimmerian darkness of the interlunar night, exactly in the same way I know that a gloriously brilliant chapter will also come after the endless reproach and humiliation of the neglected humanity of today. Those who love humanity, those who desire the welfare of all living beings, should be vigorously active from this very moment, after shaking off all lethargy and sloth, so that the most auspicious hour arrives at the earliest.

...This endeavor, the well-being of the human race, concerns everyone—it is yours, mine, and ours. We may afford to ignore our rights, but we must not forget our responsibilities. Forgetting our responsibilities implies the humiliation of the human race."

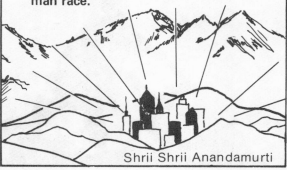

Shrii Shrii Anandamurti

"Ahimsa": Non-injury to living beings

All the aforementioned practical considerations (health, economy, etc.) are not the only reasons for not eating meat. One of the most important reasons is that we should not take life, even animal life, unnecessarily. Many religious and spiritual groups have advocated a vegetarian diet, because of the sacredness of all life and the need to live without causing suffering. According to their view, a true human being views animals not as slaves and food, but as younger brothers and sisters, and feels we have no right to cause them agony and brutally take their lives unless our survival absolutely depends upon it. Since it is possible for us to live *more* healthy lives without ever eating meat, it is appropriate to ask whether meat eating is a moral and humane habit. Clearly animals do not give up their lives willingly so that we can have the luxury of eating their flesh.

Anyone who has visited a slaughter house can testify to the fact that animals suffer greatly before and during their slaughter. In the United States alone nearly *9 million* creatures are slaughtered *daily* for our supposed dietary needs. Those of us who would weep if our dog or cat were killed go on silently condoning the needless slaughter of millions of animals each day.

A great contemporary spiritual leader, Shrii Shrii Anandamurti, explains "ahimsa" in this way: "As far as possible, articles of food are to be selected from amongst the sets of items where development of consciousness is comparatively little, i.e., if vegetables are available, animals should not be slaughtered. Secondly, before killing any animals having developed or underdeveloped consciousness, consider over and over whether it is possible to live in a healthy body without taking such lives."

Many other great saints have shared this view. During the early days of the Christian movement, for example, a large number of Christian and Jewish sects opposed meat eating as a costly and cruel luxury. Throughout history wise people and spiritual leaders have counseled that we will never be able to evolve to higher states of consciousness or create a human society based on love, until we give up the brutal habit of eating meat:

> "It is my view that the vegetarian manner of living, by its purely physical effect on the human temperament, would most beneficially influence the lot of mankind."
>
> Albert Einstein

"Animals are my friends . . . and I don't eat my friends."

"This is dreadful! Not only the suffering and death of animals, but man suppresses in himself, unnecessarily, the highest spiritual capacity — that of sympathy and pity towards living creatures like himself — and by violating his own feelings, becomes cruel."

George Bernard Shaw

55

"Truly man is the king of beasts, for his brutality exceeds them. We live by the death of others. We are burial places! I have since an early age abjured the use of meat, and the time will come when men will look upon the murder of animals as they now look upon the murder of men."

Leonardo da Vinci

"While we ourselves are the living graves of murdered animals, how can we expect any ideal conditions on the earth?"

Leo Tolstoy

"World peace, or any other kind of peace, depends greatly on the attitude of the mind. Vegetarianism can bring about the right mental attitude for peace...it holds forth a better way of life, which, if practiced universally, can lead to a better, more just, and more peaceful community of nations."

U Nu, former
Prime Minister of Burma

What is the "vital life principle?"

The "Vital Life" principle states that certain foods contain more life force (prana) than others. The importance of vitality in foods was appreciated 2500 years ago by Pythagoras, who said, "Only living, fresh foods can enable man to apprehend the truth." The Russian novelist Tolstoy said, "Feeding upon the carcass of a slain animal has something of a bad taste about it."

We know that all life lives on energy from the sun, and this energy is stored inside green plants, fruits, nuts, grains, and vegetables. When we eat these, we consume the solar energy directly. In other words, we feed on "live" food with almost all the vital energy still intact. Many plants retain their life-giving energy for many days after they are picked; in fact, they remain still capable of sprouting and growing. Meat, on the other hand, has been in process of decay for several days. For thousands of years yogis and sages have taught that both mind and body are profoundly influenced by what we eat. "You are what you eat" is a saying that applies to both body and mind. According to one yogi, "The human body is constituted of innumerable living cells...The nature of your living cells will be formed in accordance with the type of food you take.

Ultimately these together will affect your mind to some extent. If the cells of the human body grow on food, rotten and bad smelling from the flesh of animals in which mean tendencies predominate, it is but natural that the mind will lean more towards meanness."

Actually, the word "vegetarian" does *not* come from 'vegetable' but rather from the Latin word *vegetare*, which means "to enliven." When the Romans used the term *homo vegetus*, they referred to a vigorous and dynamically healthy person; yet people today think of a vegetarian as a vegetable eater.

Some famous vegetarians...

Albert Einstein, Plato, Leo Tolstoy, Bob Dylan, Louisa May Alcott, Susan St. James, Henry David Thoreau, Ralph Waldo Emerson, Benjamin Franklin, Richard Wagner, Socrates, Alexander Pope, Ovid, Sir Isaac Newton, H. G. Wells, Pythagoras, Candice Bergen, Mahatma Gandhi, Rabindranath Tagore, Horace Greeley, Leonardo da Vinci, Clement of Alexandria, Buddha, Dick Gregory, John Wesley, Voltaire, Jean Jacques Rousseau, John Milton, Charles Darwin, General William Booth, Plutarch, Paul Newman, Seneca, Albert Schweitzer, Percy Bysshe Shelley, Dr. J. H. Kellogg, St. Francis, Clint Walker, Upton Sinclair, James Coburn, George Bernard Shaw, Dalai Lama.

I still like the taste of meat —

What shall I do?

An ancient yogic principle suggests that the best way to change a deeply embedded habit is NOT to "pull it out by the roots" (a nearly impossible task), but rather to plant, nurture and cultivate an opposing habit next to the old one—and to give the new habit a lot of care, love and attention (like cultivating a mental rose bush). Very soon this new habit will grow strong and beautiful, and, with hardly an effort, the old weed, i.e., the flesh eating habit, will wither and drop out of sight. Here are some suggestions for cultivating your new "rose bush:"

● Buy two or three vegetarian cookbooks* and keep them where you will see them often (this is a great money saving strategy—an imaginative, delicious, high protein vegetarian diet can cut the average food bill by 50%).

● Learn one or two easily prepared vegetarian dishes and substitute them occasionally for a meat dinner.

*See page 62.

● Visit a natural foods store, your local food co-operative, or food buying club. Look around and ask questions.

● Call your local Ananda Marga Center and tell them you would like to visit and observe during cooking hours. (Ananda Marga is an international social service and meditation organization.)

The task of changing from a carnivorous diet to a diet of living, fresh, nutritious foods is much easier than it might initially seem. There are literally thousands of highly nutritious, tasty dishes we non-vegetarians have never had the opportunity to sample due to habit, conditioning, and lack of information. Most people are astonished to discover so many high protein dishes made from ingredients they are totally unfamiliar with—millet, buckwheat, groats, garbanzo beans, lentils, brown rice, and tofu, to name a few. Remember, learning vegetarian cooking is probably far, far easier than you may imagine. Many beginners report enjoying cooking for the first time in their lives. An unexpected delight of vegetarian cooking is the fact that after learning a few basic principles (with a good cookbook as a guide) one can easily apply them to a seemingly endless number of grains, legumes, vegetables, and nuts.

If all else fails in your efforts to become

a vegetarian, take an afternoon off and visit a slaughterhouse—this will be all the encouragement you need.

You can expect some difficulty in making the transition in the beginning, but not nearly as much as in quitting smoking, for instance. Most people find the immediate rewards (higher energy level, cleaner digestive system, increased mental clarity, sweeter body odor) so gratifying that the process of change becomes an exhilarating experience. The radiant health that comes is not only physical; you will feel the joy of putting humanitarian ideals into action and the happiness that comes from performing a service of love to all the creatures (human and non-human) of this planet. Eating a vegetarian diet, the natural diet for human beings, does the least harm to living creatures on our planet, and it helps us become more and more aware of the unity of life and realize the One Infinite Consciousness that underlies everything.

Cooking for Consciousness is the most complete and practical vegetarian cookbook on the market in this author's opinion. Designed for the beginner, it provides literally everything one needs to know in order to make the transition: what to buy, where to buy it, how to start. The recipes, whether exotic and international, hearty main dishes or easy-to-make pastries, are unmatched on the market of natural foods cookbooks for flavor and reliability. It is available at your local bookstore or natural food store, or send $6.95 plus $1.00 postage and handling to:

Ananda Marga Publications, Box M
854 Pearl Street
Denver, Colorado 80203
(303) 832-6465

Additional copies of this book are also available from the above address. Send $2.05 plus $0.65 shipping and handling.

62

Bibliography

The following books and articles are the major sources of information for this book.

A Guide to Human Conduct, Shrii Shrii Anandamurti, Ananda Marga Publications.

"A Vegetarian Manifesto," Frances Moore Lappe, in *Ramparts,* June 1973.

"Atheriosclerotic Disease: an Anthropologic Theory," W.S. Collins, in *Medical Counterpoint,* December 1969.

Eating for Life, Nathaniel Altman.

"Food First," Frances Moore Lappe and Joseph Collins, in *Renaissance Universal Journal,* Fall, 1976.

The Great Universe, Shrii Shrii Anandamurti, Ananda Marga Publications.

The Health Secrets of a Naturopathic Doctor, M.O. Garten.

"Here's What You Should Know About Vegetarianism," Grotta-Kurska, in *Today's Health,* October 1974.

"Is There Really A Food Shortage?," John Powell, in *Northwest Passage,* April-May 1974.

"The Morality of Meat," Andy Clark, in *Portland Scribe,* March 1975.

"The Next Crisis: Universal Famine," Michael T. Malloy, in *National Observer,* March 30, 1974.

Protein for Vegetarians, Gary and Steve Null.

PROUT - A New Ideology for a New Era, Prout Publications.

"Summary of Results of Adventist Mortality Study, 1958-65," School of Health, Loma Linda University.

"Vegetarianism: A Force Against Famine?," C.E. Fager, in *Christian Century,* October 29, 1975.

INDEX